When God Was All Alone

Words by Norman C. Habel
Pictures by Jim Roberts

P A PURPLE PUZZLE TREE BOOK

COPYRIGHT © 1971
CONCORDIA PUBLISHING HOUSE,
ST. LOUIS, MISSOURI
CONCORDIA PUBLISHING HOUSE LTD.,
LONDON, E. C. 1
MANUFACTURED IN THE
UNITED STATES OF AMERICA
ISBN 0-570-06500-3

Concordia Publishing House

A long, long time ago
when God was all alone,
He had no one to talk with
and He had no one to play with.
He had no one to live with
and He had no one to stay with.

So that wasn't any fun,
now was it?

A long, long time ago
when God was all alone,
the world was like a fishbowl
full of dirty water,
and not one little fish.

So that wasn't any fun,
now was it?

A long, long time ago
when God was all alone,
there wasn't any green
and there wasn't any white.
There wasn't any yellow
and there wasn't any light.
But everything was purple,
a very dirty purple,
from the dirty purple water.

So that wasn't any fun,
now was it?

Then the water started churning,
churning round and round,
and it made a funny sound,
like **chuuuurple**

chuuuurple chuuuurple

But that wasn't very good,
now was it?

So God looked in the water
to see what He could see.
But He couldn't see a thing
except a dirty purple.
For there wasn't any light
and there wasn't any green.
There wasn't any yellow
and there wasn't any white.

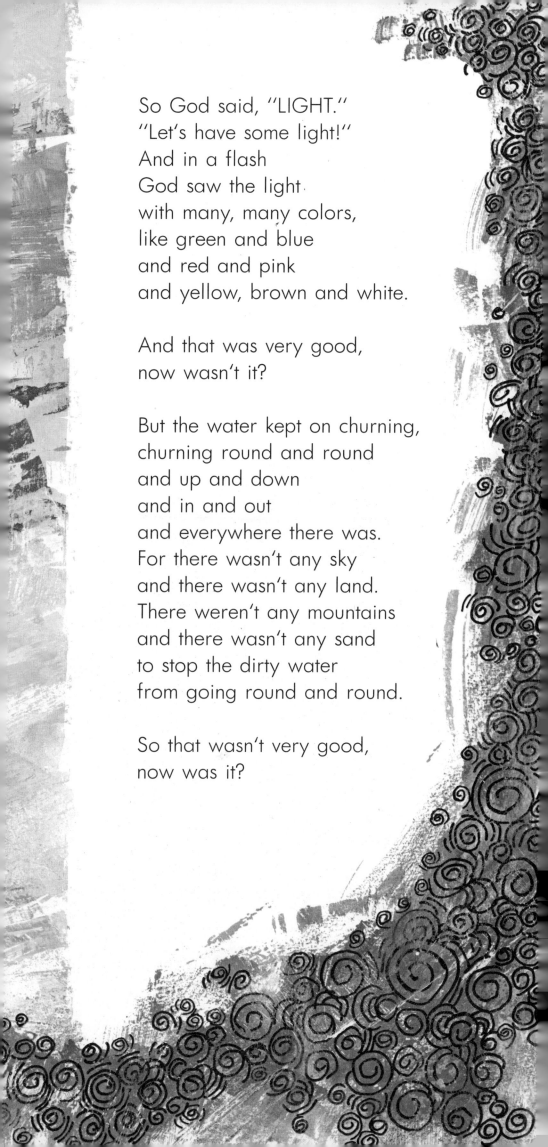

So God said, "LIGHT."
"Let's have some light!"
And in a flash
God saw the light
with many, many colors,
like green and blue
and red and pink
and yellow, brown and white.

And that was very good,
now wasn't it?

But the water kept on churning,
churning round and round
and up and down
and in and out
and everywhere there was.
For there wasn't any sky
and there wasn't any land.
There weren't any mountains
and there wasn't any sand
to stop the dirty water
from going round and round.

So that wasn't very good,
now was it?

EEEE

So God said, "LAND."
"Let's have some land!"
And in a flash
there was a hump,
a very lumpy hump,
a bumpy, lumpy, humpy hump,
that came between the water.
And it stopped the dirty water,
the water that was purple,
from churning round
and up and down
and in and out
and making funny sounds
like

chuuuurple
chuuuurple chuuuurple

The hump was made of sand
and dirt and rocks
and grass and trees.
And so God called it "land."

The land was brown
and dark and green.
It hardly makes a sound.
But sometimes it says,

EEEEEEEEEEEEEEEEEEEEEEEEEEEEEEEEEEEEEEEEEEEEEEEEEEEE

if you put your ear down to the ground
and listen late at night.

Then God said, "SKY."

"Let's have some sky!"

And in a flash
there was a ceiling,
very, very high,
over all the land.
That ceiling stopped the water,
that water up above us,
from falling down
and going round
and everywhere there was.

So that was very good,
now wasn't it?

The ceiling God called "sky,"
for it is very high.
But no one really knows
just how high it goes!
Do you?

Then in that sky God hung some stars
and once in a while an old one falls.
From that ceiling way up there
God swung two yellow balls,
the sun by day
and the moon by night.
But neither of them falls
when He swings them out of sight.

Then God said, "LIFE."
"Let's have some life
to fill the land and sky!"
Then in a flash
there was a splash
as purple fish went swimming.
And after this
there was a swish
as birds and gnats went zooming.
Then after a while
God had to smile
as He watched the animals
learning how to walk.

So God made everything there was.
He made the ants
and he made the snails
and the clumsy kangaroos
who have very funny tails,
the purple fish
and the old black crows
and the camel with a hump
and the happy hippopotamus,
who has very dirty feet
that make a funny sound
like phump shluuuurphump
shluuuurphump

So that was very good,
now wasn't it?

So God made everything there was
and He had so much fun.
For He loved that world and all He made
and said, "That's very good."

And that was
very, very good!
Now wasn't it?

OTHER TITLES

SET I.
WHEN GOD WAS ALL ALONE 56-1200
WHEN THE FIRST MAN CAME 56-1201
IN THE ENCHANTED GARDEN 56-1202
WHEN THE PURPLE WATERS CAME AGAIN 56-1203
IN THE LAND OF THE GREAT WHITE CASTLE 56-1204
WHEN LAUGHING BOY WAS BORN 56-1205
SET I. LP RECORD 79-2200
SET I. GIFT BOX (6 BOOKS, 1 RECORD) 56-1206

SET II.
HOW TRICKY JACOB WAS TRICKED 56-1207
WHEN JACOB BURIED HIS TREASURE 56-1208
WHEN GOD TOLD US HIS NAME 56-1209
IS THAT GOD AT THE DOOR? 56-1210
IN THE MIDDLE OF A WILD CHASE 56-1211
THIS OLD MAN CALLED MOSES 56-1212
SET II. LP RECORD 79-2201
SET II. GIFT BOX (6 BOOKS, 1 RECORD) 56-1213

the PURPLE PUZZLE TREE